Harpo Speaks . . . about New York

Harpo Speaks . . . about New York
by
Harpo Marx

with Rowland Barber

With an Introduction
by
E. L. Doctorow

THE LITTLE BOOKROOM
New York

© 1961 by Harpo Marx and Rowland Barber
Introduction © 2000 by E. L. Doctorow

Reprinted from Harpo Speaks!
by permission of Proscenium Publishers Inc., New York
Design: Katy Homans, Homans Design, New York
Cover: Harpo Marx on his Bar Mitzvah day
Photo courtesy of William Marx
Drawings (endpapers and opposite): Susan Marx

The publisher gratefully acknowledges the generosity and assistance of
Susan Marx, William Marx, Melvyn Zerman, and Matthew Lore

Library of Congress Cataloging-in-Publication Data
Marx, Harpo, 1888–1964.
Harpo speaks . . . about New York / by Harpo Marx with Rowland Barber
p. cm.
ISBN 1-892145-06-5
1. Marx, Harpo, 1888–1964—Childhood and youth. 2. Comedians—United
States—Biography. 3. Motion picture actors and actresses--United States—
Biography. I. Title.
PN2287.M54 A3 2001
791.43'028'092—dc21
[B]   00-060643

First Printing May 2001

THE LITTLE BOOKROOM
5 St. Luke's Place
New York NY 10014
212.691.3321 • Fax 212.691.2011
bookroom@rcn.com

Introduction

E. L. DOCTOROW

Like all city children of my generation I revered the Marx Brothers. I don't recall bothering to understand why they were so funny but I looked forward to each of their movies for what I knew would happen: they would dismantle any society in which they found themselves. Everywhere they went they brought chaos and confusion. Nothing could stop them.

Groucho, Chico, and Harpo may not have been the only comedians to outrage propriety, violate custom, and make a shamble of the hope of human dignity, but they disdained the dramatized self usage of a Keaton or a W. C. Fields, offering instead the brazen assertion of themselves as Marx brothers no matter what names were assigned to them by their screenwriters. Always they stood outside the milieu of their movies, heaping verbal or physical abuse on any character actor who had the misfortune to serve as their foil. They were unremitting surrealists.

Even their musical interludes—Chico at his piano, Harpo at his harp—had no discernable dramatic justification. What made them the most radical of their profession was that their comedy, unmediated by anything like normal sentiment, went to the root of the vital social pretense that life is purposeful and the universe subject to reason.

Had we not had the Marx Brothers at the opera, at the races, aboard ship, or at war, I think there would have been perhaps less understanding from us in later life of such exemplars of Modernism as Giorgio de Chirico, Marc Chagall, Luis Buñuel, and Samuel Beckett.

Though Zeppo Marx occasionally appeared as a straight man, as far as we children were concerned there were just the three brothers. Chico we liked the least—perhaps because he was the least funny, or his characterization was thinnest, or because we detected something slipshod or false in his performances. Groucho, we acknowledged, was the wit. He had the words, he sang the songs, and was usually conniver of the plot and the organizer of things (though in the true and anarchic spirit of the Marx Brothers, their alliances were subject to instant revision and the other two as often as not might make him the victim of their slapstick). But there were moments when we felt menaced by Groucho, as if there was some darkness in him, or some inadvertent revelation of the sadistic lineaments of adulthood that was perhaps premonitory of our own darkness of spirit as when we laughed guiltily at his ritual abasement of the statuesque, maternal Margaret Dumont.

Where Harpo was concerned, there were no reservations. He was our favorite. He was the Marx brother we truly loved. Groucho may have had command of the language, and Chico as well, under the constraints of his oddly chosen Italian accent, but Harpo, in speaking not at all, was our spokesman.

Harpo communicated by putting his knuckles to his teeth and whistling, or by honking the car horn he pulled from his voluminous pockets. When the situation was dire he could warn Chico with a charade. When a pretty girl walked by, his remarkably pliant face—the glazed-over eyes, the dropped jaw—told us everything we needed to know in that split second before he took up the chase. Speechless, he was the purest clown of the three. His wig, his crushed top hat, and those depthless pockets that gave forth scissors, saws, lighted lamps, working telephones, kitchen utensils, and dead chickens, were the trappings of a genius kid. We too were sometimes the proud possessors of what the world thought of as junk. We too had that swiftness of foot that would allow us to chase girls and manage never to catch them. We too understood everything there was to know about the adult world . . . but said nothing.

We loved Harpo because instinctively we knew he was one of us. But we couldn't have understood that his own life as a child might have been the reason for our recognition. In fact the creative depth of his clowning had to have come from something more profoundly ingrained in his nature than his adult experience in the theater as one of the Marx Brothers about to hit it big in Hollywood. It is impossible to believe that the first time Harpo hung his knee on the hand of the startled distinguished actor standing next to him, that it was a planned routine. It had to have been the inspired improvisation of someone who had grown up in the street, as Harpo did in the streets of New York in the raucous 1890s where survival depended on one's precise stance toward authority. The Marx Brothers' movies are all about outwitting authority. But apparently it was the gleeful Harpo, the family's street urchin so constantly in its presence, who learned to hustle it with a goofy leer, and make it the inadvertent minion of his own surreal authority.

Handing your leg to a distinguished person is a not inconceivable metaphor for someone, like Harpo, who as a kid had only one ice skate to skate on. Making a comic routine out of a wealth of found objects in your pockets has a certain resonance if as a boy you sustained yourself by selling to junk dealers the treasures you found in the street or stole from moving vans.

The world young Harpo had to outwit included not only cops, truant officers, and neighborhood toughs, but also his family's impoverishment, and a degree of distraction from his loving parents that allowed him to drop out of school in the second grade. He had to outwit the New York of his day that gave to such children of immigrants as Adolph "Harpo" Marx a tenement airshaft in which to hang his Christmas stocking, and the luxury of attending New York Giants baseball games on a hill outside the ballpark from which he could see only the left fielder.

The reader will find no self-pity in these memories—they are related with the humor of someone who long ago arose from them into a triumphant professional life. But Harpo's stories make it clear that in his critical early years the world never quite assembled itself from the fractured understandings of his experience into anything comfortably ordinary or rational. The city of New York was in that day an atonality of immigrant cultures, with adjoining blocks ringing with different languages. Children who wandered into streets not their own were routinely mugged. The homes of the rich abutted the homes of the poor. Brewery owners stood in for aristocracy as their liveried carriages clattered over the cobblestone past the awed gaze of urchins. New York was a raucous municipal democracy in which citizenship was not a requirement for voting. The most exciting holiday of the year was not Christmas, but Election Day because it was celebrated by the lighting of enormous bonfires in the middle of every street in every neighborhood.

A collage of disparate, violently yoked together elements, New York was the surreal composition of a mad artist. Perhaps in some instinctive way Adolph Marx understood that and it led to his deliverance. Or else why, as Harpo, would he remember so fondly . . . his watch with no hands . . . his lone ice skate . . . the wedge of outfield grass in the Polo Grounds . . . or the old warped harp that had been his grandmother's . . . standing in a corner as if waiting for him?

Harpo Speaks . . . about New York

How I came to be educated, over the years, I don't exactly know. I only know that it didn't happen during my sojourn at New York City Public School No. 86.

When the century turned in 1900, people tried to begin the new century with a clean slate. Some people forgave old debts. Some cleaned their slates by having their names changed. Others did it by giving up rye whiskey, cuss words, or snuff. The New York City Board of Education did it by promoting Adolph Marx to the second grade.

This was a noble gesture, but it didn't work. The year and a half Adolph Marx spent in Grade Two was more of a waste of time and taxpayers' money than the year he spent drifting and dreaming through Grade One.

(Adolph is the name I was given when I was born, in New York City, in 1893. Harpo is the name I was given during a poker game twenty-five years later.

During the same game my brother Leonard became "Chico," Julius became "Groucho," Milton "Gummo," and Herbert later became "Zeppo." Those handles stuck from the moment they were fastened on us. Now it's like we'd never had any other names. So we will be known all the way through these pages as Chico, Harpo, Groucho, Gummo and Zeppo.)

Anyway, my formal schooling ended halfway through my second crack at the second grade, at which time I left school the most direct way possible. I was thrown out the window.

There were two causes of this. One was a big Irish kid in my class and the other was a bigger Irish kid. I was a perfect patsy for them, a marked victim. I was small for my age. I had a high, squeaky voice. And I was the only Jewish boy in the room. The teacher, a lady named Miss Flatto, had pretty much given up on teaching me anything. Miss Flatto liked to predict, in front of the class, that I would come to no good end. This was the only matter on which the Irish kids agreed with Miss Flatto, and they saw to it that her prediction came true.

Every once in a while, when Miss Flatto left the room, the Irishers would pick me up and throw me out the window, into the street. Fortunately our room was on the first floor. The drop was about eight feet—high enough for a good jolt but low enough not to break any bones.

I would pick myself up, dust myself off, and return to the classroom as soon as I was sure the teacher was back. I would explain to Miss Flatto that I had been to the toilet. I knew that if I squealed I'd get worse than a heave out the window. She must have believed I didn't have enough sense to control my organs, let alone comprehend the subjects of reading and writing. She began sending notes to my mother, all with the same warning: something had better be done about straightening me out or I would be a disgrace to my family, my community, and my country.

My mother was too busy with other matters at the time to straighten me out with the public school system. For one thing, it seemed more urgent to keep my older brother Chico out of the poolroom than to keep me in the schoolroom.

So my mother appointed a delegate to go confer with Miss Flatto. That was unfortunate. The delegate was the boy friend of my cousin Polly, who was then living with us. He peddled herring in the streets, out of wooden buckets, yelling up and down the neighborhood, "Hey, best here! Best here! Best here in de verld!" Naturally, he stunk from fish; you could smell him a block away.

So one day he turned up in the middle of a class, fish buckets and all. He didn't get very far in his conference with Miss Flatto. She took one look and one smell, began to get sick, and ordered Polly's boy friend to leave the school. All the other kids in the room began to smirk, holding their noses, and Miss Flatto did nothing to stop them.

I knew I was dead.

The two Irish boys now gave me the heave-ho every chance they got, which was three or four times a day, and Miss Flatto made me stay after school every afternoon for leaving the room so many times without permission. I can still see her finger waggling at the end of my nose, and hear her saying, "Some day you will realize, young man, you will realize!" I didn't know what she meant, but I never forgot her words.

So one sunny day when Miss Flatto left the room and I was promptly heaved into the street, I picked myself up, turned my back on P. S. 86 and walked straight home, and that was the end of my formal education.

I was eight years old when I was thrown out of school the last time. Home at that time was a flat in a tenement at 179 East 93rd Street, in a small Jewish neighborhood squeezed in between the Irish to the north and the Germans to the south in Yorkville.

The tenement at 179 was the first real home I can remember. Until we moved there we had lived like gypsies, never traveling far—in fact never out of the neighborhood—but always moving, haunted and pursued by eviction notices, attachments, and glinty-eyed landlord's agents. The Marxes were poor, very poor. We were always hungry. And we were numerous. But thanks to the amazing spirit of my father and my mother, poverty never made any of us depressed or angry. My memory of my earliest years is vague but pleasant, full of the sound of singing and laughter, and full of people I loved.

The less food we had, it seemed, the more people we had to feed. Nobody grumbled about this. We just worked a little harder and schemed a little harder to hustle up a soup bone or a pail of sauerkraut. There were ten mouths to feed every day at 179: five boys, from Chico down to Zeppo, cousin Polly, who'd been adopted as one of us; my mother and father, and my mother's mother and father. A lot of the time my mother's sister, Aunt Hannah, was around too. And on any given night of the week, any given number of relatives from both sides of the family might turn up, unannounced but never unwelcome.

A Relative was anybody who was named Schoenberg or Marx or who spoke Plattdeutsch who turned up in our flat at dinnnertime and caused the portions on our plates to diminish. A lot of suspicious-looking strangers became Relatives, but nobody was ever turned away.

This put all kinds of burdens on Frenchie, which is what we called my father, Sam Marx. Frenchie was the family housekeeper and cook. He was also the bread-winner. Frenchie was a tailor by trade. He was never able to own his own shop, and during the day his cutting table and sewing bench took up the whole dining room with lengths and scraps of materials overflowing into the kitchen. At six o'clock he quit whatever he was working on, in the middle of a stitch, and stashed his profession in the hall, materials, tools, tables and all, and turned to the task of making dinner for ten or eleven or sixteen people.

This task would have been hopeless to anybody else in the world, but Frenchie always managed to put a meal on the table. With food he was a true magician. Given a couple of short ribs, a wilting cabbage, a handful of soup greens, a bag of chestnuts and a pinch of spices, he could conjure up miracles. God, how fabulous the tenement smelled when Frenchie, chopping and ladling, sniffing and stirring and tasting, and forever smiling and humming to himself, got the kitchen up to full steam!

Frenchie was born in a part of Alsace-Lorraine that had stayed loyal to Germany, even when France ruled the province. So while the official language was French, at home the Marxes spoke "Plattdeutsch," low-country German.

When the family came to America, they naturally gravitated toward immigrants who spoke the same dialect. On the upper East Side of Manhattan (on the border of Yorkville, just as Alsace-Lorraine was on the border of Germany), a sort of Plattdeutsch Society sprang up—unofficial, but tightly knit.

Anybody who spoke Plattdeutsch was okay with Frenchie, had his undying trust. And since Frenchie was one of the few tailors in the city who spoke Plattdeutsch he got a lot of business, out of sheer sentiment, that he never deserved. If it weren't for the mutual loyalty of Frenchie and his landsmen, the Marx brothers wouldn't have stayed under the same roof long enough to have become acquainted, let alone go forth into show business.

Of all the people Frenchie loved and was loyal to, none was more unlike him than Minnie Schoenberg Marx, his wife, my mother. A lot has been written about Minnie Marx. She's become a legend in show business. And just about everything anybody ever said about her is true. Minnie was quite a gal.

She was a lovely woman, but her soft, doelike looks were deceiving. She had the stamina of a brewery horse, the drive of a salmon fighting his way up a waterfall, the cunning of a fox, and a devotion to her brood as fierce as any she-lion's. Minnie loved to whoop it up. She liked to be in the thick of things, whenever there was singing, storytelling, or laughter. But this was in a way deceiving too. Her whole adult life, every minute of it, was dedicated to her Master Plan.

Minnie's Plan was simply this: to put her kid brother and her five sons on the stage and make them successful. She went to work down the line starting with Uncle Al (who'd changed his name from Schoenberg to Shean), then took up, in order, Groucho, Gummo, myself, Chico and Zeppo. This was one hell of a job. What made it even tougher was the fact that only Uncle Al and Groucho wanted to be in show business in the first place, and after Groucho got a taste of the stage, he wanted to be a writer. Chico wanted to be a professional gambler. Gummo wanted to be an inventor. Zeppo wanted to be a prize fighter. I wanted to play the piano on a ferryboat.

But nobody could change Minnie's mind. Her Master Plan was carried out, by God, all down the line.

Her relationship with Frenchie, in the days when I was growing up, was more like a business partnership than the usual kind of marriage. Minnie was the Outside Man. Frenchie was the Inside Man. Minnie fought the world to work out her family's destiny. Frenchie stayed home, sewing and cooking. Minnie was the absolute boss. She made all the decisions, but Frenchie never seemed to resent this.

It never occurred to us that this setup between mother and father was odd, or unnatural. We were like a family of castaways surviving on a desert island. There was no money, no prestige, no background, to help the Marxes make their way in America. It was us against the elements, and each of us found his own way to survive. Frenchie took to tailoring. Chico took to the poolroom. I took to the streets. Minnie held us all together while she plotted our rescue.

The only tradition in our family was our lack of tradition.

So anyhow, at the age of eight, I was through with school and at liberty. I didn't know what to do with myself. One thing was certain: I'd never go near P. S. 86 or come within range of Miss Flatto's wagging finger again. School was okay for Chico, who was in the fifth grade and a whiz at arithmetic, and Groucho, who was knocking off 100's in the first grade, but not for me. I was good only at daydreaming, a subject they didn't give credit for in the New York City school system.

My parents accepted my being at liberty like they accepted every other setback in their lives—no remorse, no regrets. Minnie was too busy engineering Uncle Al's career to have much time for me. She felt she had done her duty anyway, by sending Polly's herring-peddler boy friend around to the school. Frenchie took the news of my quitting with a shrug and a nodding smile.

I never knew for sure, but I suppose the truant officer must have come around to our flat looking for me. If he did, I know what happened. When he knocked we assumed it was the landlord's agent, come to collect the rent, and we all ran to our hiding places and kept quiet until we heard the footsteps go back down the stairs outside.

As for myself, I never doubted I had done the right thing when I walked away from the open window of P. S. 86, never to return. School was all wrong. It didn't teach anybody how to exist from day to day, which was how the poor had to live. School prepared you for Life—that thing in the far-off future—but not for the World, the thing you had to face today, tonight, and when you woke up in the morning with no idea of what the new day would bring.

When I was a kid there really was no Future. Struggling through one twenty-four-hour span was rough enough without brooding about the next one. You could laugh about the Past, because you'd been lucky enough to survive it. But mainly there was only a Present to worry about.

Another complaint I had was that school taught you about holidays you could never afford to celebrate, like Thanksgiving and Christmas. It didn't teach you about the real holidays like St. Patrick's Day, when you could watch a parade for free, or Election Day, when you could make a giant bonfire in the middle of the street and the cops wouldn't stop you. School didn't teach you what to do when you were stopped by an enemy gang—when to run, when to stand your ground. School didn't teach you how to collect tennis balls, build a scooter, ride the El trains and trolleys, hitch onto delivery wagons, own a dog, go for a swim, get a chunk of ice or a piece of fruit—all without paying a cent.

School didn't teach you which hockshops would give you dough without asking where you got your merchandise, or how to shoot pool or bet on a poker hand or where to sell junk or how to find sleeping room in a bed with four other brothers.

School simply didn't teach you how to be poor and live from day to day. This I had to learn for myself, the best way I could. In the streets I was, according to present-day standards, a juvenile delinquent. But by the East Side standards of 1902, I was an honor student.

Somehow, between home and out ("out" being any place in the city except our flat), I learned to read.

While Groucho sweated over copybook phrases like "This is a Cat—O, See the Cat!" and "A Penny Saved Is a Penny Earned," I was mastering alphabet and vocabulary through phrases like "This water for horses only," "Exclesior Pool Parlor, One Cent a Cue," "Saloon and Free Lunch—No Minors Admitted," "Keep off the Grass," and words printed on walls and sidewalks by older kids which may not be printed here.

I learned to tell time by the only timepiece available to our family, the clock on the tower of Ehret's Brewery at 93rd Street and Second Avenue, which we could see from the front window, if Grandpa hadn't pulled the shade. Grandpa, who was the last stronghold of orthodox religion in the family, often used the front room to say his prayers and study the Torah. When he did, and the shade was drawn, we had to do without the brewery clock, and time ceased to exist.

I've had, ever since then, the feeling that when the shades are pulled, or the sun goes down, or houselights dim, time stops. Perhaps that's why I've never had any trouble sleeping, and why I've always been an early riser. When the sun is out and the shade is up, the brewery clock is back in business. Time is in again, and something might be going on that I'd hate to miss.

Minnie's mother, Fanny Schoenberg, died soon after we moved to East 93rd Street, but Grandpa Schoenberg remained a figure in the household until he finally resigned from living at the age of one century, in 1919. Grandpa was therefore not classified as a Relative. He was Family.

Weekdays, when Minnie was out hustling bookings for Uncle Al, Frenchie was busy over his cutting table, Chico and Groucho were in school, and Gummo and Zeppo were down playing on the stoop, Grandpa and I spent a lot of time together.

Sometimes he'd tell me stories from the Haggadah, lecture me from the Torah, or try to teach me prayers. But his religious instruction, I'm afraid, was too close to schoolwork to interest me, and he didn't accomplish any more with me than Miss Flatto did. Still, without realizing it, I completed a course. From Grandpa I learned to speak German. (I tried to teach Grandpa English, but gave up on it.)

When he was feeling chipper and the shade was

up, Grandpa used to perform magic for me. He conjured pennies out of his beard, and out of my nose and ears, and made me practice the trick of palming coins. Then he would stoke up his pipe and tell me about the days when he and Grossmutter Fanny toured the German spas and music halls. Grandpa performed as a ventriloquist and a magician, in the old country, while Grandma played the harp for dancing after he did his act.

I hadn't known Grandma too well before she died, but I felt she was never far away, for Grandma's old harp stood always in a corner of Grandpa's room. It was a half-size harp. Its strings were gone. Its frame was warped. All that remained of its old luster were a few flakes of golden dandruff. But to me it was a thing of beauty. I tried to imagine what it must have sounded like when Grandma played it, but I couldn't. I had never heard anybody play a harp. My head was full of other kinds of music—the patter songs of Uncle Al, the bagpipes of St. Patrick's Day, the drums and bugles of Election Day, the calliope on the Central Park carousel, zithers heard through the swinging doors of Yorkville beer gardens, the concertina the blind man played on the North Beach excursion boat. But I'd never heard a harp.

I could see Grandma with the shining instrument on her lap, but in my daydreams no sound came forth when her hands touched the strings.

I made a resolution, one of the few I can remember making. I was going to get a job and save my money and take the harp to a harp place and have it strung and find out at last what kind of music it made.

When I did earn my first wages, however, I found more urgent ways of spending the dough. It was to be nearly fifteen years before I plucked my first harp string. I was not disappointed. It was a thrill worth saving.

So at any rate, Grandpa, who taught me German and magic, was my first real teacher. My second teacher furthered my education in a much more practical way. This was my brother Chico.

My brother Chico was only a year and a half older than me, but he was advanced far beyond his age in the ways of the world. He had great self-confidence, like

Minnie, and like her he rushed in where Frenchie or I feared to tread.

I was flattered when people said I was the image of Chico. I guess I was. We were both of us shrimps compared to the average galoots in the neighborhood. We were skinny, with peaked faces, big eyes, and mops of wavy, unruly hair. Pop was no better at cutting our hair than he was at cutting material for a suit.

Chico was a good teacher, and for him I was a willing student. In a short time he taught me how to handle a pool cue, how to play cards and how to bet on the dice. I memorized the odds against rolling a ten or four the hard way, against filling a flush in pinochle or a straight in poker. I learned basic principles, like "Never go against the odds, at any price," and "Never shoot dice on a blanket." I learned how to spot pool sharks and crooked dealers, and how to detect loaded dice.

I spent more time in the poolroom, and the price of pocket billiards had risen from a penny a cue to two for a nickel. That was big money. An evening's pool cost more than I usually managed to bring home from a day's hustling, doing odd jobs and hocking whatever loose merchandise I might chance to find lying around.

What took really big money was the Special Dinner at Fieste's Oyster House. Dining at Fieste's was the supreme luxury of my young life. Not that the food there was any better cooked than the food we had at home—when we had food. No common commercial chef could ever compete with Frenchie. But Fieste's Special included things that Frenchie could only dream of putting on our table: Greenpoint oysters and cherrystone clams on the half shell, deviled crab, grilled smelts, French fried potatoes and onions, a juicy T-bone steak, hot rolls soaked with butter, apple pie with a slab of sharp cheese, and coffee rich with thick, sweet cream.

As I said, a meal like this took really big money. It cost thirty-five cents.

I soon learned what the main pitfall was in saving money. It wasn't temptation, or the lack of will power. It was Chico Marx. Chico could smell money. Hiding my savings at home, anywhere in the flat, was useless. Chico always found it sooner or later.

Once I thought I had him outsmarted. I sold a

wagonload of junk over on the West Side, items I had selected off a moving van hitched in front of a house on 90th Street. The junk dealer gave me ten cents cash, the most I ever made on a single wagonload.

I swore that this dime would not wind up in Chico's pocket. For once I was sure it wouldn't because I had finally found the perfect hiding place. In our bedroom there was a small tear in the wallpaper, near the ceiling. Before Chico came home that night I stood on the dresser and pasted my dime to the wall under the flap of the torn paper. It was a slick job. I went to bed with a feeling of security.

Next morning when I got up there was a bigger rip in the paper than before. My dime was gone and so was Chico. Chico was the only person I ever knew who could smell money through wallpaper. Maybe he didn't have much of an ear for music, but he had a hell of a nose for currency.

So I learned that the only way to protect my money was to spend it as fast as I earned it. I also learned to spend it on something I could eat, or use up, like dinner at Fieste's or a game of pool. My possessions were no safer from Chico's clutches than my money. Chico was a devout believer in the maxim "Share and share alike."

The way he shared my possessions was to hock them as fast as he got his hands on them, and then give the pawn tickets to me as my share.

Life in the streets was a tremendous obstacle course for an undersized kid like me. The toughest obstacles were kids of other nationalities. The upper East Side was subdivided into Jewish blocks (the smallest one), Irish blocks, and German blocks, with a couple of Independent Italian states thrown in for good measure. That is, the cross streets were subdivided. The north-and-south Avenues—First, Second, Third and Lexington— belonged more to the city than the neighborhood. They were neutral zones. But there was open season on strangers in the cross streets.

If you were caught trying to sneak through a foreign block, the first thing the Irishers or Germans would ask was, "Hey, kid! What Streeter?" I learned it saved time and trouble to tell the truth. I was a 93rd Streeter, I would confess.

"Yeah? What block 93rd Streeter?"

"Ninety-third between Third and Lex." That pinned me down. I was a Jew.

The worst thing you could do was run from Other Streeters. But if you didn't have anything to fork over for ransom you were just as dead. I learned never to leave my block without some kind of a boodle in my pocket—a dead tennis ball, an empty thread spool, a penny, anything. It didn't cost much to buy your freedom; the gesture was the important thing.

It was all part of the endless fight for recognition of foreigners in the process of becoming Americans. Every Irish kid who made a Jewish kid knuckle under was made to say "Uncle" by an Italian, who got his lumps from a German kid, who got his insides kicked out by his old man for street fighting and then went out and beat up an Irish kid to heal his wounds. "I'll teach you!" was the threat they passed along, Irisher to Jew to Italian to German. Everybody was trying to teach everybody else, all down the line. This is still what I think of when I hear the term "progressive education."

I took to spending a lot of time in Central Park, four blocks to the west, the park being a friendly foreign country. It was safe territory for lone wolves, no matter what Streeters we were.

Summers I hung around the tennis courts. I loved to watch the game, and there was always the chance I would hustle myself a tennis ball. In the wintertime the park was not so inviting, unless there'd been a snowfall or a good freeze. When there was snow on the ground I'd hustle a dishpan somewhere ("hustle" being a polite word for steal), and go sliding in the park. This was a risky pleasure. A dishpan in good condition was worth five cents cash from a West Side junk dealer, and I had more than one pan swiped out from under me by bigger kids.

After a freeze they would hoist the Ice Flag in Central Park, which told the city the pond was okay for skating. Nobody was happier to see the flag than I was. I was probably the best single-foot skater in New York City.

Our family's total sports equipment was one ice skate, which had belonged to Grandma, and which Grandpa kept as a memento, like the old harp. And as the harp had no strings, the skate had no straps. I had to improvise with twine, rope, old suspenders, elastic bands, whatever I could find.

I spent many hours on the frozen pond in Central Park, skating gimpily around the edge of the ice on my one left-foot skate. I spent many more hours sitting on the ice, freezing my bottom where my pants weren't patched, tying and splicing and winding in the endless struggle to keep the skate lashed to my foot.

Oddly enough, winter had fewer hardships for me than summer did. I could always find a warm spot somewhere when it was cold. But when the city was hot, it was hot through and through, and there was no cool spot to be found.

The only relief was temporary, like a chunk of ice from the loading platform of the ice works. That was a blessing to hold and suck on, but it didn't last long. What to do then? Only one thing to do then—go for a swim in the East River. But the way we had to swim, off the docks, was exhausting and we couldn't stay very long in the water.

You can always spot a guy who grew up poor on the East Side by watching him go for a swim. When he gets in a pool he will automatically start off with a shallow kind of breast stroke, as if he were pushing away some invisible, floating object. This was a stroke you had to use when you jumped in the East River. It was the only way you could keep the sewage and garbage out of your face.

One way of keeping your mind off the heat was making horsehair rings. We used to sneak into the brewery stables and cut big hanks of hair from the horses' tails, then braid them into rings. Horsehair rings were not only snazzy accessories to wear, three or four to a finger, but they were also negotiable. They could be swapped for marbles or Grover Cleveland buttons, and they were handy as ransom when you were ambushed by an enemy gang.

Then, suddenly one summer, rings and marbles became kid stuff to me. I found out how to use the city transportation system for free, and I was no longer a prisoner of the neighborhood. My life had new horizons. I, a mere mortal, could now go forth and behold the Gods in Valhalla—which is to say, the New York Giants in the Polo Grounds.

Trolleys were the easiest way to travel without paying. You just hopped on board after a car had started up, and kept dodging the ticket taker. If the ticket taker caught up with you, you got off and hopped on the next trolley to come along. It was more sporting to hang on the outside of the car, but you took a chance of being swatted off by a cop.

It wasn't so easy with elevated trains. You couldn't get on an El train without giving a ticket or transfer to the ticket chopper at the platform gate. To swindle the ticket chopper took a good deal of ingenuity, involving old transfers, chewing-gum cards (which happened to be the same size as tickets), some fancy forgery—and for me, thanks to Grandpa's training—sleight of hand.

Once a year the city would change its system of tickets and transfers, trying to cut down on the number of free riders. But they never came up with a system that couldn't somehow be solved by us kids.

Thus I was now a man-about-town. In my travels I found out, in the summer of 1903, how to watch the Giants play for free. That was the only sure way to beat the heat in New York. When John J. McGraw and his noble warriors took the field in the Polo Grounds, all the pains and complaints of the loyal fan faded away, and he sweltered in blissful contentment.

I was a loyal fan but I could never afford, naturally, the price of admission to the Polo Grounds. Then I discovered a spot on Coogan's Bluff, a high promontory behind the Polo Grounds, from which there was a clear view of the ballpark. Well, a clear view—yes, but clear only of the outside wall of the grandstand, a section of the bleachers, and one narrow, tantalizing wedge of the playing field.

So to tell the truth, I didn't really watch the Giants. I watched a Giant—the left fielder.

When the ball came looping or bounding into my corner of the field, I saw real live big-league baseball. The rest of the time—which was most of the time—

I watched a tiny man in a white or gray uniform standing motionless on a faraway patch of grass.

Other kids collected pictures of Giants such as McGraw, McGinnity and Matthewson. Not me. I was forever faithful to Sam Mertes, undistinguished left fielder, the only New York Giant I ever saw play baseball.

Eventually I came to forgive Sam for all the hours he stood around, waiting for the action to come his way. It must have been just as frustrating for him down on the field as it was for me up on the bluff. It was easy for pitchers or shortstops to look flashy. They took lots of chances. My heart was with the guy who was given the fewest chances to take, they guy whose hope and patience never dimmed. Sam Mertes, I salute you! In whatever Valhalla you're playing now, I pray that only right-handed pull-hitters come to bat, and the ball comes sailing your way three times in every inning.

Much as I ran away from it every chance I got, the home neighborhood was not altogether a dreary slum.

It had its share of giants too, men and women who belonged to the Outside World, who brought glitter and excitement into the lives of the rest of us East Siders.

Such were two true aristocrats in our neighborhood, Mr. Ruppert and Mr. Ehret, the owners of the big breweries. Jake Ruppert's mansion was on the corner of 93rd and Park Avenue. This was a fabulous place to me, for the principal reason that Ruppert's garden contained a row of peach trees, which once a year bore lovely, luscious peaches.

Ruppert's garden also contained two huge watchdogs who ranged along the inside of the iron spiked fence, on the alert for peach poachers. It was the theory of Ruppert's caretaker that the dogs would be more vicious if they were kept hungry. This theory backfired. I used to hustle a bag of fat and meat scraps from a butcher, feed the starving dogs through the fence until they got friendly and sleepy, then shinny over the spikes and fill my shirt with ripe peaches.

No fruit ever tasted so sweet as stolen fruit, which

was about the only kind I ever had until I became, at the age of eleven, a full time working man.

There was spectacular pageant on our street, every weekday of the year. The show went on at nine in the morning, and was repeated at six in the evening. This was the passing of Mr. Ehret through 93rd Street, to and from the Ehret Brewery.

Mr. Ehret rode in a dazzling black carriage, pulled by a team of prize black stallions. A footman and a coachman, in regal uniforms of blue and gold, sat on top of the carriage. The eastern half of our block sloped downhill toward the East River and when the brewer's carriage reached the top of the slope, in the morning, the coachman would stand up and shake the reins and the stallions would charge down the hill in full gallop.

When they passed our house, the stallions were wild-eyed and foaming at their bits, and the cobblestones rang like anvils. When they returned at night, straining against the rise, you could see the sparks fly up from their pounding hooves.

Thunder and lightning. Pomp and circumstance. Glory and magnificence. I wonder how a poor kid who never watched a brewer ride to the brewery, who never shivered with goose bumps when the coachman rose to start the downhill gallop, could ever know that there was another kind of life, the Good Life.

Thanks for the show, Mr. Ehret. Thanks for the peaches, Mr. Ruppert. Sorry I never liked beer.

Then there were the Brownstone People. They weren't as high and mighty as the brewers, but I think they furthered my education about the outside world just as much.

We lived on the tenement side of 93rd Street, the north side. Facing us, on the south, was a row of one-family brownstone town houses. They were not cluttered in front with ugly fire escapes, like the tenements. They were decorated with ivy and window-boxes full of flowers.

What went on inside those elegant houses was something I found impossible to imagine, like the sound of harp music. While other kids wondered about life on Mars or on the Moon, I used to wonder about life across the street. For hours at a time, I watched the Brownstone People come and go.

At Christmastime, the brownstones across the street were even more remote from my tenement world. Wreaths of holly appeared on the doors and in the windows, and at night I could see Christmas trees inside, glowing with the lights of candles.

The one thing I remembered that Miss Flatto had taught me, in P. S. 86, was the legend of Santa Claus. I was entranced by it, but being a young cynic, I told myself it was all a bunch of Irish malarkey. The only time anybody got presents in our family was when Uncle Al came to visit or when Frenchie happened to get paid for two suits at a crack.

Nevertheless, on the night of December 24, a month after my ninth birthday, I decided to give Santa Claus a chance to make good. I hung one of my stockings in the airshaft, pinned under the window. The airshaft, I figured, was the nearest thing to a chimney in our house. Maybe even better. A lot more room for a fat and jolly old guy to shinny down.

On Christmas morning my stocking was still

empty. I didn't tell anybody about it. I was too ashamed of being played for a sucker.

Yet, a year later, when I saw the holly on the brownstones, and the candles flickering on the Christmas trees, I swallowed my pride and hung my stocking again. This time, to bolster my faith, I confessed to Chico that night what I had done. Chico wasn't scornful, or even surprised. He knew all about the Christmas stocking deal. "But," he said, "you got to figure the odds. Figure how many airshafts on 93rd Street, let alone the rest of the city, Sandy Claus has to shinny down in one night. Then you figure he's got to take care of the Irishers and Bohunks and Eyetalians before he gets around to the Jews. Right? So what kind of odds is that?"

Chico was being sensible and convincing as usual. Still, it was a question of faith versus mathematics. A stubborn glimmer of faith still burned inside me. I left my stocking in the airshaft.

Next morning Chico surprised me. He got to the stocking before I did. When he found it empty, he was disappointed and he was sore. He wadded up the stocking and threw it at me. "When are you going to learn?" he said. "When are you going to learn you can't go against the odds?"

The only holidays we shared as a family were the excursions we took, once every summer, to the beach. We couldn't afford to go as far as the ocean, out at Coney Island. We took the cheaper excursion boat from the dock at 96th Street, the one that paddled up through Hell Gate to North Beach, in the Bronx.

At North Beach we had a marvelous time, basking in the sweet air of freedom. We were where no freeloading relatives or rent agents or disgruntled customers of Frenchie's could ever find us. Minnie told jokes and sang songs with Groucho, Frenchie snoozed on the sand, smiling even in his sleep, and Chico would wander off looking for some action. I was supposed to mind Gummo and Zeppo, but I ducked away every chance I got to see if I could hustle a charlotte russe or a hunk of watermelon off some kid smaller than me.

Our feast for the holiday would be a stack of sandwiches, liverpaste and cheese on stiff pumpernickel bread. The cheese was green, and so hard it had to be spread with a paint scraper, but it was delectable.

We would stretch the day to the last possible minute, running—along with the rest of the crowd—to catch the last boat home. By the time the warped old tub chugged back into the East River, all the passengers would be on one side, leaning wearily toward home, and the boat would list until you could reach your hand over the rail and skim the scum off the river. It was a miracle every time it made the dock and got itself hitched to the piles and pulled up level before capsizing.

It was always a melancholy homecoming. For most of us on board, the one-day excursion was the only vacation we would have from a year of hard work and misery. The blind man who played the concertina knew there wasn't another nickel or penny left for his tin cup amongst the whole crowd, but he played on, and sang homesick Italian ballads.

In the boat's saloon there was a piano, bolted with iron straps to the deck. Its keyboard was locked. The piano must have been left over from the boat's palmier days, when the passengers wore white flannels and linens, and there was an orchestra for dancing. Nobody ever played the piano on our excursions, and that was the sad part of the holiday for me.

At thirteen I attained manhood, according to the Jewish faith. I was bar mitzvah—inducted as an adult member of the synagogue. This didn't mean, however, that I would start going to shul every Saturday. The rites were performed out of deference to Grandpa, who would have been bitterly hurt if his grandsons hadn't shown this much respect for their traditional faith. It was the least we could do.

For the occasion, Frenchie made me a black serge knee-breeches suit (pieced together of unsold "lappas") and bought me a derby hat. After the ceremony there was a reception for me at 179 with a spread of sweets, pastries and wine. This, naturally, attracted all the relatives, and it was quite a party. I received four presents. Uncle Al gave me a pair of gloves. Aunt Hannah gave me a pair of gloves. Cousin Sam gave me a pair of gloves. (In my bar mitzvah photograph I'm wearing two pairs, one over the other, and holding the third.)

Minnie, bless her, gave me a genuine, one-dollar Ingersoll watch.

The inevitable happened. Three days after my bar mitzvah, my new watch was missing.

I was pretty damn sore. A present was not the same as something you hustled. I tracked down Chico to a crap game and asked him what about it. He handed me the pawn ticket. I gave the ticket to Minnie and she reclaimed the watch for me. Then a brilliant idea occurred to me. I would show Chico. I would make my watch Chico-proof, so he couldn't possible hock it again. I removed its hands.

Now the watch was mine forever. I wound it faithfully each morning and carried it with me at all times. When I wanted to know what time it was I looked at the Ehret Brewery clock and held my watch to my ear. It ran like a charm, and its ticking was a constant reminder that I had, for once, outsmarted Chico.

There was one supreme holiday every two years, and there was nothing sad about it. This was not a family affair. It belonged to everybody. The poorest kid in town had as much a share in it as the mayor himself.

This was Election Day.

Months ahead, I started, like every other kid, collecting and stashing fuel for the election bonfire. Having quit school, I could put in a lot of extra hours at it. I had a homemade wagon, a real deluxe job. Most kids greased their axles with suet begged or pinched off a butcher shop, but I was fancier. I scraped genuine axle grease off the hubs of beer wagons, working the brewery circuit from Ehret's to Ruppert's to Ringling's.

I hauled staves, slats, laths, basket-lids, busted carriage spokes, any loose debris that would burn, and piled it all in a corner of our basement. This was one thing the janitor helped me with. The Election Day bonfire was a tradition nobody dared to break. If you were anti-bonfire you were anti-Tammany and life could become pretty grim without handouts from the Organization.

The great holiday lasted a full thirty hours. On election eve, the Tammany forces marched up and down the avenues by torchlight, with bugles blaring and drums booming. There was free beer for the men, and free firecrackers and punk for the kids, and nobody slept that night.

When the Day itself dawned, the city closed up shop and had itself a big social time—visiting with itself, renewing old acquaintances, kicking up old arguments—and voted.

About noon a hansom cab, courtesy of Tammany Hall, would pull up in front of our house. Frenchie and Grandpa, dressed in their best suits (which they otherwise wore only to weddings, bar mitzvahs or funerals), would get in the cab and go clip-clop, in tip-top style, off to the polls. When the carriage brought them back they sat in the hansom as long as they could without the driver getting sore, savoring every moment of their glory while they puffed on their free Tammany cigars.

At last, reluctantly, they would descend to the curb, and Frenchie would make the grand gesture of handing the cabbie a tip. Kids watching in the streets and neighbors watching from upstairs windows were properly impressed.

About a half-hour later, the hansom cab would reappear, and Frenchie and Grandpa would go off to vote again. If it was a tough year, with a Reform movement threatening the city, they'd be taken to vote a third time.

Nobody was concerned over the fact that Grandpa happened not to be a United States citizen, or that he couldn't read or write English. He knew which side of the ballot to put his "X" mark on. That was the important thing. Besides, Grandpa's son-in-law's cousin was Sam Marx, a Big Man in the Organization. Cousin Sam had a lot to say about whose name appeared under a black star on the ballot. And it was he who made sure the carriage was sent to 179 at voting time. A man of principle, which Grandpa was, had no choice but to return the courtesy by voting.

Then came the Night. The streets were cleared of horses, buggies and wagons. All crosstown traffic stopped. At seven o'clock firecrackers began to go off, the signal that the polls were closed. Whooping and hollering, a whole generation of kids came tumbling down out of the tenements and got their bonfires going. By a quarter after seven, the East Side was ablaze.

Whenever our 93rd Street fire showed signs of dying down, we'd throw on a fresh load of wood, out of another basement, and the flames would shoot up again. After my stash was piled on the blaze, I ran upstairs to watch from our front window with Grandpa.

It was beautiful. Flames seemed to leap as high as the tenement roof. The row of brownstones across the street, reflecting the fire, was a shimmering red wall. The sky was a great red curtain. And from all over the city, we could hear the clanging of fire engines. Our bonfire never got out of hand but a lot of others did on election night.

Grandpa enjoyed the sight as much as I did, and he was flattered when I left the rest of the boys to come up to share it with him. He pulled his chair closer to the window and lit the butt of his Tammany stogie. "Ah, we are lucky to be in America," he said in German, taking a deep drag on the cigar he got for voting illegally and lifting his head to watch the shooting flames. "Ah, yes! This is a true democracy."

I had no idea what Grandpa was talking about, but he was a man of great faith and whatever he said was the truth.